Nip Dip Nap

Written by Catherine Baker

Collins

Dad pats it.

It nips.

nip nip

It sips.

sip sip

It is in.

Nap!

It naps.

pads

pat

nap

13

It sits, it nips, it naps

 Review: After reading

Use your assessment from hearing the children read to choose any GPCs or words that need additional practice.

Read 1: Decoding
- Ask the children to read the following. Check that they sound talk and blend as they read the words aloud. Then ask them to copy you as you mime each word.

  pats **nips** **dip** **nap**
- Read page 2. Ask the children to point to the word that begins with the /m/ sound. (**mat**) Read page 3. Ask the children to point to the word that begins and ends with the /d/ sound. (**Dad**)
  - Ask: Can you blend in your head silently before reading these words aloud?

Read 2: Prosody
- Turn to page 8 and point to the exclamation mark. Explain that this means we must read with extra feeling.
  - Say: I'm going to use a commanding voice as if the girl is telling the lizard to have a nap. Read and then ask the children to have a go.
- On page 9, ask: What feeling shall we put in our voice? Discuss how pleased we might be that it is having a nap at last. Model reading **It naps.** and then encourage the children to read the sentence in a happy or relieved voice.

Read 3: Comprehension
- Talk about what it might be like to have a pet lizard. Ask: Would patting a lizard feel the same as patting a pet cat? What else might be different?
- Use the pictures on pages 14 and 15 to model how to recap the content of the book. Encourage the children to have a go.
- Bonus content: Ask the children to describe each picture on pages 10 and 11. Can they find the pages earlier in the book that show a lizard sitting, napping and being patted?
- Bonus content: Discuss the lizard life cycle shown in the pictures on pages 12 and 13. Explain how the adult lizard lays eggs which hatch into young lizards, and then the young lizards grow into adults and lay eggs.